13 Colonies

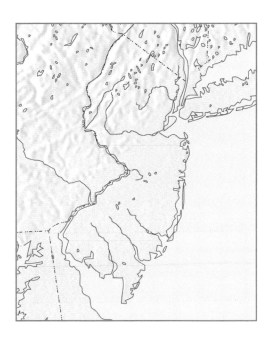

NEW JERSEY

13 Colonies

NEW JERSEY

The History of New Jersey Colony, 1664–1776

ROBERTA WIENER AND JAMES R. ARNOLD

Raintree

Chicago, Illinois

For information, address the publisher:
Raintree, 100 N. LaSalle, Suite 1200, Chicago, IL 60602

Printed and bound in China

08 07 06 05 04
10 9 8 7 6 5 4 3 2 1

Library of Congress Cataloging-in-Publication Data
Wiener, Roberta, 1952-
    New Jersey / Roberta Wiener and James R. Arnold.
        p. cm. -- (13 colonies)
Summary: A detailed look at the formation of the colony of New Jersey, its government, and its overall history, plus a prologue on world events in 1664 and an epilogue on New Jersey today.
Includes bibliographical references and index.
    ISBN 0-7398-6883-7 (lib. bdg.) -- ISBN 1-4109-0307-9 (pbk.)
    1. New Jersey--History--Colonial period, ca. 1600-1775--Juvenile literature. 2. New Jersey--History--Revolution, 1775-1783--Juvenile literature. [1. New Jersey--History--Colonial period, ca. 1600-1775. 2. New Jersey--History--Revolution, 1775-1783.] I. Arnold, James R. II. Title. III. Series: Wiener, Roberta, 1952-   13 colonies.
    F137.W67 2004
    974.9'02--DC21
                        2003011058

Title page picture: The scenic Great Falls of the Passaic River at the site of present-day Paterson, NJ.

Opposite: An early New Jersey settlement.

The authors wish to thank Walter Kossmann, whose knowledge, patience, and ability to ask all the right questions have made this a better series.

Some words are shown in bold, **like this.** You can find out what they mean by looking in the glossary.

Picture Acknowledgments

Authors: 58-59 Anne S.K. Brown Military Collection, Brown University Library, Providence, RI: 55 bottom Colonial Williamsburg Foundation: 6, 12, 29, 30 top, 34, 38 bottom, 48 U.S. Government Printing Office: Cover, 56 bottom Historical Society of Pennsylvania: 23, 44 *Howard Pyle's Book of the American Spirit*, 1923: 19, 24, 57 Independence National Historical Park: 25 bottom, 55 top left and top right Eric Inglefield: 58 inset, 59 inset Library Company of Philadelphia: 17, 28, 33, 49 Library of Congress: 5, 7, 9, 10-11, 26, 27, 30 bottom, 31, 32, 36, 37, 39, 42 National Archives: 40 top, 47, 56 top New Jersey Historical Society: 21 top, 43, 52-53, 54 I. N. Phelps Stokes Collection, New York Public Library: Title page, 14 Rare Books Division, New York Public Library: 40-41 Courtesy of the Special Collections of the Newark Public Library: 21 bottom, 22, 50-51 Courtesy of the North Carolina Office of Archives and History: 13, 16, 38 top, 45 Philadelphia Free Library: 25 top

Contents

PROLOGUE: THE WORLD IN 1664

In 1664, the year the English took possession of New Jersey, at least 75,000 Europeans lived in England's North American **colonies**. Well-established colonies already existed to the north and south of New Jersey. The **Dutch** considered New Jersey to be part of New Netherland, their colony immediately to the north. To the south lay the former colony of New Sweden, founded in Delaware in 1638, and then taken over by New Netherland in 1655.

Nearly two centuries of exploration and colonization by European nations preceded England's acquisition of New Jersey. Europe had begun to explore the world

COLONY: A LAND OWNED AND CONTROLLED BY A DISTANT NATION; A COLONIST IS A PERMANENT SETTLER OF A COLONY

The world according to a European mapmaker around 1570

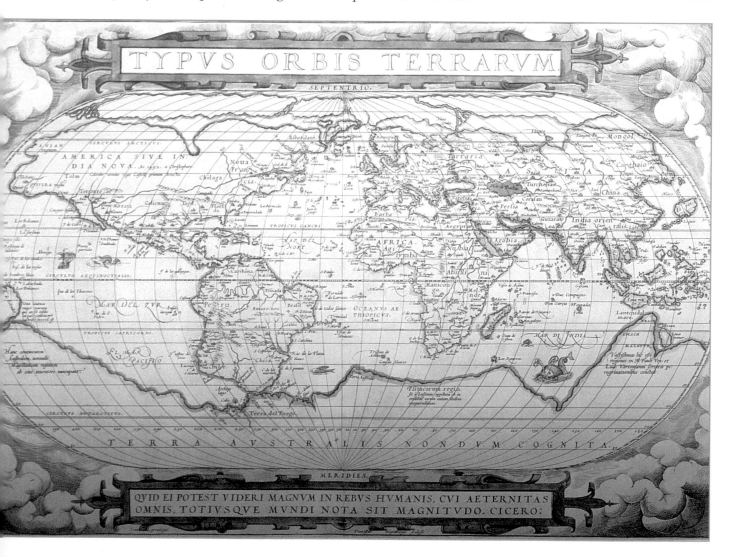

DUTCH: NATIONALITY OF PEOPLE BORN IN THE NETHERLANDS

during the Renaissance, a period of invention and discovery. Advances in navigation and the building of better sailing ships allowed longer voyages. So began the Age of Exploration, with great seamen from Portugal, Spain, Italy, France, and England sailing into uncharted waters. Beginning in the 1400s, they reached Africa, India, the Pacific Ocean, China, Japan, and Australia. They encountered kingdoms and civilizations that had existed for centuries.

Europeans did not yet have a clear idea where all these lands were, but they knew enough to see great opportunities. They saw the chance to grow rich from trade in exotic spices. They saw the chance to make

Beginning in 1619, Dutch traders bought slaves in Africa and sold them on the far side of the Atlantic. They were the first to bring African slaves to an English colony in North America, Virginia.

NETHERLANDS: "LOW COUNTRIES"; A EUROPEAN NATION FORMED BY THE UNION OF SEVERAL LOW-LYING PROVINCES, INCLUDING HOLLAND. AMSTERDAM IS THE CAPITAL CITY.

Some of the routes taken by European explorers

conquests and expand their countries into great empires. And not least, they saw the dark-skinned people of Africa and, thinking they were a different species, they saw the chance to capture and sell slaves. Traders from the **Netherlands** began joining other Europeans in voyaging to Africa, Asia, and the Pacific to trade in spices and slaves. They eventually formed the Dutch East India Company.

The voyages from Europe to these distant shores went around Africa. This made the trip long and dangerous. So European explorers began to sail westward in search of shortcuts. They believed a northwest passage lay somewhere to the west, and a northeast passage through the Arctic ice to the northeast. Then in 1492 the explorer

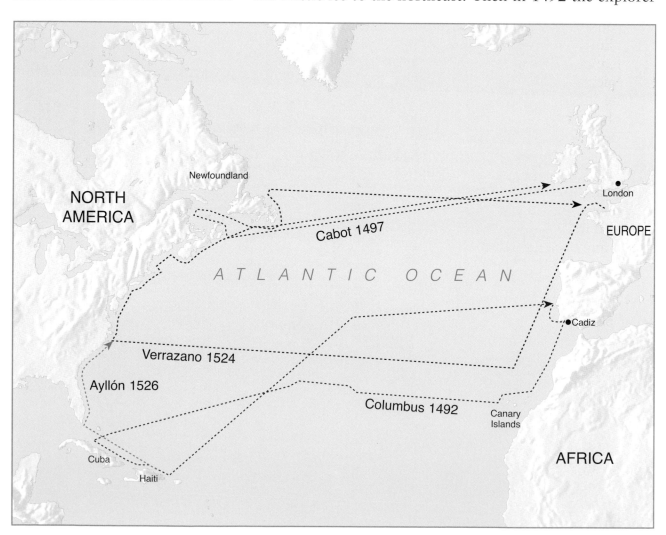

Christopher Columbus landed on an island on the far side of the Atlantic Ocean and claimed it for Spain. He thought that he had actually sailed all the way around the world and come to an island near India. Years of exploration by numerous sailors passed before the people of Europe realized that Columbus had been the first European of their era to set foot on unknown land. They called this land the New World, although it was not new to the people who lived there.

After Columbus, Amerigo Vespucci claimed to have reached the New World. Whether he actually did or not, in 1507 a mapmaker put his name on a map, and the New World became **America,** or the Americas. Still looking for a shortcut to the riches of Asia, European explorers continued to sail to North and South America. They began to claim large pieces of these lands for their own nations.

The Italian explorer, Giovanni da Verrazano, was the first European to visit the land that became New Jersey, in 1524. He was sailing in the service of France at the time, searching for a passage to Asia, and his voyage stirred France's interest in America. The French eventually established several settlements in Canada. Several French adventurers explored inland North America, including the Mississippi Valley and the land around the Great Lakes.

But the Spanish were far ahead of other Europeans in the competition for land in the Americas. Before the English came to America, the Spanish had already claimed huge portions of both North and South America. They had conquered two mighty **Native American** empires, and introduced the first domestic cattle and horses to the Americas. They founded the first two permanent cities— St. Augustine and Santa Fe—in what would become the United States. They had brought European civilization as well, including printing presses and universities. The Spanish also brought their chosen form of Christianity, Roman **Catholicism**, and converted hundreds of Native Americans, often by force.

Not until 1609, however, did another European set foot on the shore of New Jersey. Not to be outdone by the

Giovanni da Verrazano was born in Italy in 1485, and received his education there before moving to France. France provided him with ships to explore for a passage to Asia. Sailing across the Atlantic in 1524, Verrazano explored the American coast from North Carolina to New England. In 1528, he sailed across the Atlantic to Florida and the Caribbean. He went ashore on one of the islands and was eaten by cannibals.

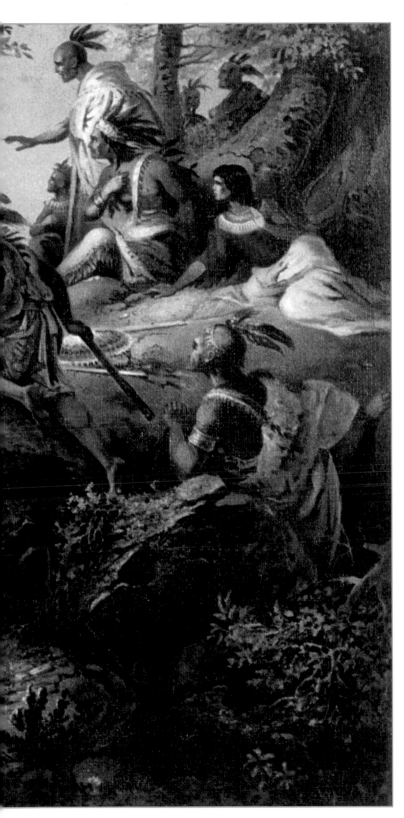

exploring sea captains of rival nations, the Netherlands joined the search for a passage to Asia when the Dutch East India Company hired the English captain, Henry Hudson. In 1609, Hudson sailed up the American river that would later bear his name. He came ashore to trade with the native people who had lived there for centuries. The Hudson River came to mark part of the boundary between the future New York and New Jersey.

In spite of decades of warfare with other European nations, including England, by 1664 the Netherlands had become a powerful nation. The **Dutch** had expelled Portugal and other rivals from territories in Africa and Asia, and had come to dominate trade with China and Japan as well as the African slave trade. However, a second war with England stripped the Netherlands of their colonial possessions in New York and New Jersey.

DUTCH: THE NATIONALITY OF PEOPLE BORN IN THE NETHERLANDS

Henry Hudson and his crew of English and Dutch sailors set out in the *Half Moon* in 1609. It was Hudson's third voyage to searche for a northeast passage to Asia. He had promised his employers that he would return to the Netherlands after exploring the Arctic. Instead he sailed the *Half Moon* across the Atlantic Ocean to Maine. From Maine, Hudson and his crew searched for a northwest passage in Chesapeake Bay, Delaware Bay, and then the Hudson River, trading with the Native Americans for furs as they went. The *Half Moon* sailed about 150 miles (241 kilometers) up the Hudson, as far as a large ship could go.

I.
ENGLAND TAKES OVER

Rivalry between England and the Netherlands was intense and sometimes erupted into war. In North America, the Dutch colony of New Netherland prevented nearby English colonies from expanding. The Dutch also competed with the English colonies for trade. So, the English decided to expel the Dutch from North America. During the second Anglo-Dutch war, a fleet of English

CHARTER: A DOCUMENT CONTAINING THE RULES FOR RUNNING AN ORGANIZATION

In 1660, King Charles II took the throne of England after years of living in exile in Europe during the English Civil War. After his death in 1685, his brother, the Duke of York, became King James II.

ships sailed into New Amsterdam's harbor and demanded that the Dutch surrender the city and the colony. The English fleet was too strong to resist, so the Dutch surrendered on August 27, 1664. New Netherland became New York, named for the king's brother, the Duke of York, and New Amsterdam became New York City. So certain were the English of victory that King Charles II had already given the duke a **charter** for the territory on March 12, 1664.

James, Duke of York, received the land he called New Jersey along with the rest of New Netherland. The Dutch argued, to no avail, that New Jersey was not included in their surrender at New Amsterdam. Before the Dutch had even surrendered, the duke decided to transfer ownership of New Jersey to his two

friends, Lord John Berkeley, and Sir George Carteret. The duke named the land "New Jersey" in honor of Carteret's service as governor of Jersey, an English-controlled island off the coast of France. Carteret sent his 26-year-old cousin, Captain Philip Carteret, to govern the province. The captain sailed across the Atlantic with about 30 English and French colonists.

Not only did Sir George Carteret own much of New Jersey, he also owned a share of the Carolinas. So did his co-proprietor, Lord John Berkeley.

2.
NEW JERSEY IN 1664

Bodies of water serve as the boundaries of New Jersey on three sides: the Hudson River and the Atlantic Ocean to the east, Delaware Bay to the south, and the Delaware River to the west. Its one land border is with New York state. The largest area of New Jersey is covered by a coastal plain, and within this plain lies the unique pine **barrens**, a land of cedar swamps and dwarf oak forests. An English visitor to the pine barrens wrote, "the barren grounds have ... the tallest and greatest pine and pitch trees that I have seen." The piedmont, or foothill, region extends from the coastal plain to the hilly northwestern corner of New Jersey. In that corner, at High

BARRENS: A TRACT OF LAND ON WHICH LITTLE CAN GROW

The scenic Great Falls of the Passaic River at the site of present-day Paterson, NJ. inspired artists.

Point, is New Jersey's highest point, only 1,803 feet (550 meters) above sea level.

For such a small area, New Jersey has a large number of major rivers, including the Hackensack, Passaic, Raritan, and Great Egg Harbor Rivers. The land benefits from plentiful rainfall and a mild climate, with slightly colder temperatures in the highlands. It was known in the mid-1600s for its "pure healthful air, and such pure, wholesome springs, rivers, and waters." The early Dutch settlers found the winters colder than they expected and the summers hotter.

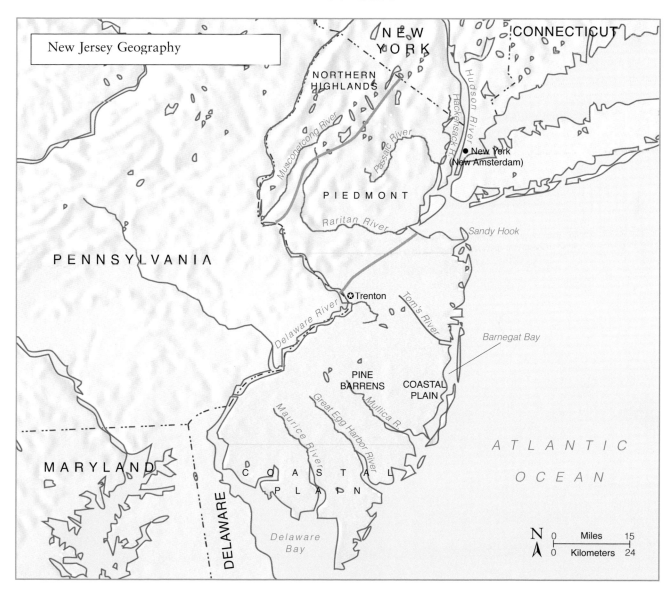

Except for a few scattered Dutch farms, trading posts, and forts along the Delaware and Hudson Rivers, New Jersey was Native American country in 1664. The Dutch settlers and traders had purchased the small plots of land on which they lived from the Leni Lenape, or Delaware, Native Americans. Trails wound through the woods from river to river and from inland villages to the seacoast. Deer, bear, and wolves roamed the land, along with numerous smaller animals, such as foxes, squirrels, skunks, raccoons, otters, and beavers. The mammals

A visitor to New Jersey reported that wild turkeys weighing as much as 46 pounds had been shot there. Turkeys were native to the Americas and were introduced to Europe.

provided skins and furs, as well as meat, while large geese and turkeys provided ample fowl. The rivers and oceans held a multitude of fish. The Native Americans lived in the interior for much of the year, but camped by the ocean in the summers to gather and feast on shellfish.

The name of the Delaware River and Bay, which defined part of the New Jersey border, came from Lord De La Warr, the second English governor of Virginia. Although the English explorer Henry Hudson had sailed a Dutch ship into Delaware Bay in 1609, it was the Virginia explorer, Samuel Argall, who sailed into Delaware Bay the following year and gave it an English name. Argall named it after his governor, and his name stuck, not only to the bay, but to a river, a colony, and an entire group of Native Americans.

A Delaware chief speaks to his people.

Henry Hudson was the first European to meet the Leni Lenapes, soon to be known as the Delawares. The Delawares were Algonquian-speakers, related to the Mahicans to the north and the Nanticoke, Conoy, and Powhatan people to the south. The Delawares were a large and powerful made up of several subgroups, including the Unami and the Munsee. The Munsee Delawares lived in northern New Jersey and nearby areas of Pennsylvania and New York. The Unami Delawares lived in southern New Jersey and Delaware. Both Munsee and Unami Delawares lived during part of the year in longhouses made of poles and bark, each holding about 100 people. They traced their descent through their mothers. These Native Americans lived a wandering life, ranging over their territory hunting, fishing, and gathering plants. They stopped in the spring long enough for the women to plant corn, beans, and squash, as well as tobacco. They wore clothing made of animal skins, but quickly came to prefer the cloth they received in trade with the Europeans.

The Delaware Native American population was about 8,000 when the first Europeans arrived, but the Europeans brought diseases, such as smallpox and measles, to which the Native Americans had never been exposed. The Delawares died by the thousands in at least seven **epidemics** that occurred during the 1600s. In the 1640s a brutal war broke out between the Munsee Delawares and New Netherland. As many as a thousand Native Americans perished in what was called Governor Kieft's War, which ended by treaty in 1645. By 1700 only about 3,000 Delawares remained.

Peter Stuyvesant, director general of New Netherland, extended his colony's reach to Delaware and forced the Swedish to surrender to him in 1655. However, Governor Kieft's War had made the interior of New Jersey a dangerous place for Dutch people. Travelers risked being ambushed by Native Americans. For the most part, the government of New Netherland ignored New Jersey and communicated with Delaware via ships sailing down the Atlantic coast from the capital at New Amsterdam, present-day New York City. However, Dutch settlers did establish the town of Bergen, at the site of present-day Jersey City, in 1660. They also mined copper in the northern highlands of New Jersey during the 1660s.

EPIDEMIC: WIDESPREAD OUTBREAK OF CONTAGIOUS DISEASE

3.
THE BUYING AND SELLING OF THE JERSEYS

Governor Philip Carteret arrives in New Jersey.

Soon after New Jersey came under English ownership, English people began settling there. Colonel Richard Nicholls, serving the Duke of York as governor of New York, had not yet heard that the duke no longer owned New Jersey. Messages took several months to travel across the ocean. Nicholls gave people permission to settle on New Jersey lands, thinking he was acting according to his orders. **Quakers** from Long Island, **Puritans** from Connecticut, and Baptists from Rhode Island all purchased land from the Native Americans and founded towns in New Jersey. Nicholls promised the New Jersey towns religious freedom, self-government, and seven years free of rent payments.

Elizabethtown, Shrewsbury, Middletown, Woodbridge, and Piscataway were the earliest towns of English New Jersey. When Governor Philip Carteret's ship arrived in 1665, he chose the new town of Elizabethtown, founded by Puritans, as the capital. The Puritans had arranged their towns so that the settlers lived close together around the town center and farmed tracts of land surrounding the town. This design was similar to towns in

New England. The New England settlers also brought with them the **town meeting** as the basis of local government. Governor Carteret accepted the presence of the Dutch settlers of Bergen. He permitted them to stay and to keep their land, and granted them an official charter for their town.

In 1666, Robert Treat led a group of Puritans from New England to found a settlement. The group members believed that the New England church was not strict enough. The Puritans sailed from New Haven, Connecticut, down the Long Island Sound. They chose to build their settlement a

Opposite: Tavern at the village of Woodbridge, New Jersey

TOWN MEETING: BASIS OF LOCAL GOVERNMENT IN NEW ENGLAND, IN WHICH VOTING CITIZENS MET AND CONDUCTED TOWN BUSINESS AS A GROUP

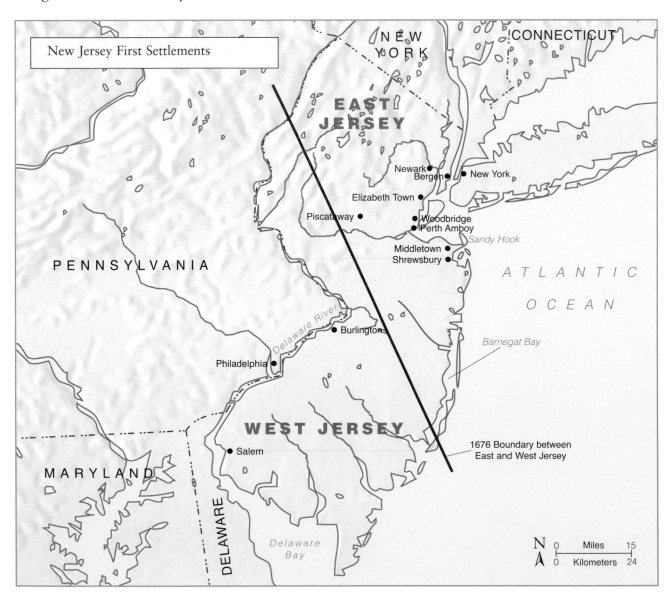

New Jersey First Settlements

NEW YORK
CONNECTICUT
EAST JERSEY
Newark
Bergen
New York
Elizabeth Town
Piscataway
Woodbridge
Perth Amboy
Sandy Hook
Middletown
Shrewsbury
PENNSYLVANIA
ATLANTIC OCEAN
Delaware River
Burlington
Barnegat Bay
Philadelphia
WEST JERSEY
1676 Boundary between East and West Jersey
Salem
MARYLAND
DELAWARE
Delaware Bay

N
0   Miles   15
0   Kilometers   24

few miles from the coast, at what became Newark, New Jersey. They stayed near the coast because they feared the Native Americans who lived inland. Their church had a watchtower, so that armed guards could watch over the church during worship. The Puritans purchased the land for their town from the native peoples, paying with such goods as guns, lead, gunpowder, clothing, tools, and liquor.

Below: In Puritan Newark, the beating of a drum signaled the start of a public work day, when all men had to pitch in to do such chores as build roads or clear fields.

The two **proprietors** of New Jersey, George Carteret and Lord Berkeley, wanted to attract settlers to their new colony and collect money by renting the land. Each settler was to receive up to 50 acres in exchange for a yearly rental of about a penny per acre. Carteret and Berkeley drew up a document granting freedom of religion and government by representatives elected to an **assembly**. The first New Jersey assembly met in 1668. Like many of the other colonies, New Jersey had a governor, an appointed council, and an elected assembly. The proprietors themselves never visited their colony.

However, many settlers, especially those who had received their land from New York's Governor Nicholls, disliked not being able to purchase the land and own it. In 1672, rebellious settlers who refused to pay rent held a meeting and declared that Philip Carteret was no longer their governor. Instead they elected Sir George Carteret's son, James, whom they thought they could control. Philip Carteret set sail for England to ask the proprietors for

The Puritans' church in early Newark had a watchtower, so that armed guards could look out for a possible lNative American attack.

help. This rebellion was interrupted by another war between England and the Netherlands. New Jersey spent a year under Dutch control before being returned to the English by treaty. With the return of the English, New Jersey's proprietors restored Philip Carteret to the governorship of New Jersey in 1674. Backed by orders from the Duke of York himself, Carteret insisted that all settlers pay their rent.

THE DIVISION OF NEW JERSEY

Lord Berkeley decided to sell his half interest in New Jersey in 1674. A new deed divided the province into East

The proprietors' seal of the colony of New Jersey, and the signatures of Carteret and Berkeley, the first two proprietors, and Edward Byllynge, a later proprietor. A proprietary colony differed from a royal colony in that the proprietors owned the land. A colony's proprietor had the right to sell or rent the land and, in some colonies, the right to make laws and run the government.

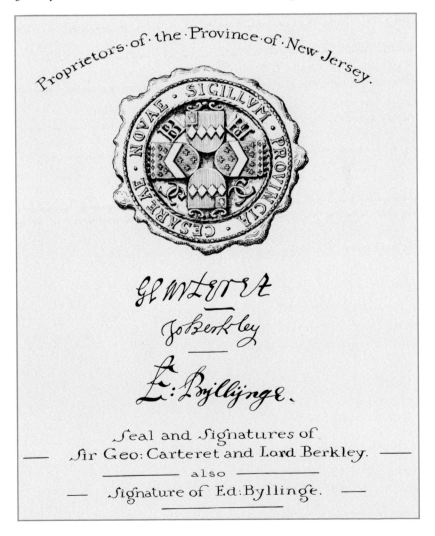

Seal and Signatures of
Sir Geo: Carteret and Lord Berkley.
also
Signature of Ed: Byllinge.

and West Jersey. Sir George Carteret kept ownership of East Jersey, while Lord Berkeley sold West Jersey to two Quakers, John Fenwick and Edward Byllynge. Fenwick and Byllynge disagreed over the division of the land, so the well-respected Quaker, William Penn, was asked to settle the dispute and divide the land between the two.

Both Fenwick and Byllynge fell on hard times. In 1675, Byllynge sold his share of West Jersey to William Penn and two other Quakers. Needing cash to found a settlement in West Jersey, Fenwick sold most of his land to several Quakers, some of whom in turn transferred it to Penn and his partners. As a result, Penn's group ended up controlling much of West Jersey. This was William Penn's first involvement in an American colony. His well-known colony, Pennsylvania, was still a few years in the future.

Both Fenwick and Byllynge intended to establish a Quaker colony in America as a refuge from religious **persecution**. But Fenwick, who still owned a small share in West Jersey, wanted his own colony. He hurried to recruit Quaker settlers, and in the autumn of 1675 arrived with about 100 colonists. They founded the town of Salem, the first English town in West Jersey, on the eastern side of the Delaware River. Fenwick could not stay

The Society of Friends

An Englishman named George Fox founded a new Christian religion, the Friends of God, or Society of Friends, around 1650. The Friends' beliefs, behavior, and appearance set them apart from other English people and other Christians. Unlike other Christians, the Friends did not have churches, worship services, or ministers. They held meetings in simple houses, and any person could speak at any time. They believed that each person had a direct relationship with God, and so did not need a minister to help communicate with him. The Friends dressed plainly, refused to take oaths, and refused to make distinctions among social classes or use forms of respect

Mary Dyer was one of the four Quakers executed in New England.

for people in high positions. They objected to all forms of violence, including war, and refused to serve in any military group.

People mockingly called the Friends "Quakers," because their founder said they should "quake" at the word of the Lord. However, the Friends did not at first call themselves "Quakers." The Society of Friends quickly attracted many followers in England, Europe, and the American colonies. Because they stood out in a time of religious intolerance, they suffered from discrimination. English law barred Quakers from holding government offices or receiving higher education. Many were jailed for their refusal to attend Church of England services, and close to 500 died in English prisons.

The Puritans, who had split from the Church of England and founded a colony in Massachusetts, especially disliked the Quakers, some of whom had come to Massachusetts in 1656. The Massachusetts colony even executed four Quakers who had returned to the colony after being expelled. In spite of widespread persecution, the Society of Friends attracted new members in most of England's American colonies. However, many Quakers strongly desired to live in a Quaker-run colony where they could enjoy true freedom of religion. Foremost among them was William Penn.

William Penn, the well-educated son of a wealthy and prominent English family, became a Quaker at the age of 22. English authorities jailed him four times for trying to convert others to his beliefs. He could have avoided prison because his father, Admiral Sir William Penn, was a good friend of King Charles II. By serving his jail sentences, Penn won the trust of other Quakers and became one of their leaders. Admiral Penn, William's father, had loaned money to King Charles II. King Charles II's brother James, the future king of England, was the Duke of York. Admiral Penn and the Duke of York together ran England's navy department. The long family friendship allowed William Penn to play an active role in the American colonies in spite of his religion.

Above: Their simple clothing made Quakers stand out in English and colonial society.

Right: William Penn played an important role in New Jersey before he received the colony of Pennsylvania.

out of legal and financial trouble, so he finally sold his share to William Penn.

In the meantime, Penn and his group of investors planned their own colonial venture. About 200 Quakers who had purchased land in the new colony sailed for West Jersey in 1677. They purchased land from the Native Americans and founded Burlington, about 50 miles up the Delaware River from Salem. Penn and his partners published an open letter to Quakers who might want to emigrate to West Jersey. The conflicts with Fenwick had attracted widespread attention among English Quakers, so the three men tried to reassure potential settlers:

"That there is such a province as New-Jersey is certain.

"That it is reputed of those who have lived and have traveled in that country, to be wholesome of air and fruitful of soil, and capable of sea trade, is also certain … .

"As for the printed paper sometime since set forth …

New Jersey's earliest towns were located near major rivers or the ocean.

as a description of that province ... we say as to two passages in it, they are not so clearly and safely worded as ought to have been; particularly, in seeming to limit the winter season to so short a time, when on further information we hear it is some time longer."

Penn played a major role in drafting a constitution for a democratic government, "Concessions and Agreements of the Proprietors, Freeholders, and Inhabitants of West New Jersey." The document called for a council of ten commissioners chosen by the proprietors, and an elected assembly.

However, another dispute arose over the right of the proprietors to govern the land. The Duke of York insisted that he had sold only the land, not the right to govern it. Edmund Andros, the governor of New York from 1674 to 1680, tried to take over the government of New Jersey in the name of the duke. Andros dissolved New Jersey's assembly and arrested Governor Carteret. A New York jury

When King Charles II gave William Penn a colony encompassing 45,000 square miles (116,550 square kilometers) , Penn lost interest in New Jersey.

freed Carteret, and in England, William Penn convinced the duke to transfer the right to govern to the proprietors. So once again, Carteret returned to govern East Jersey, and the new Quaker proprietors assumed the government of West Jersey.

About 1,400 settlers, most of them Quakers, came to Salem and Burlington. A pamphlet, "The Present State of the Colony of West-Jersey, 1681," reported that a ship sailed to the colony from London about every three months. Passage for adults cost 5 pounds to the Delaware River landing at Burlington. Land was being offered for sale in 20,000-acre lots, which several families could purchase jointly. The pamphlet promised, "There is …

Wealthy New Jersey colonists tried to live like the English upper classes. They lived in mansions similar to the ones in England. One colonist even called himself a lord, although he had no claim to the title.

certain provision made for the Liberty of Conscience, in Matters of Religion, that all Persons living Peaceably, may enjoy the Benefit of the Religious Exercise thereof, without any Molestation whatsoever."

In 1681, after the death of Sir George Carteret, William Penn and 11 other Quakers bought East Jersey from Carteret's heirs, and nearly all of New Jersey came under Quaker control. Another 12 Quakers, some of them from Scotland, bought shares, bringing the total number of proprietors of East Jersey to 24. Only one of the 24 ever settled in New Jersey. The others sold their shares to even more people, until there were 85 proprietors! As the number of owners multiplied, so did the arguments over land distribution. Lawsuits, political struggles, and civil disorders were to be a feature of life in New Jersey for another hundred years. As in many of the American colonies,

Some upper-class English families had slaves, as this portrait shows. Even though New Jersey was a northern colony, some wealthy people had dozens of slaves, in spite of Quaker objections to slavery.

common farmers and wealthy owners of large estates took opposite sides on every political or economic question.

Penn turned his attention to his huge new colony, Pennsylvania, which he received in 1682. The Scottish Quaker Robert Barclay became governor of East Jersey. About 500 Scottish Presbyterians emigrated to East Jersey. They were fleeing religious persecution in Scotland and were attracted by New Jersey's promise of religious freedom. Scottish Presbyterians founded the town of Perth Amboy in 1683.

Twenty years after the English took over New Jersey, the colony's two provinces had a population of about 5,000 living in and around ten thriving towns and along the many rivers. The European population included wealthy landowners, small farmers, and **indentured servants**. About 300 black slaves, imported from New York and the **West Indies**, worked on the larger estates. Word of fertile farmland and religious tolerance had attracted and held not only English and Scottish Quakers, but New England Puritans, Scottish Presbyterians and Irish, Dutch, Swedish, French, and German settlers of various **Protestant** religions. Lutheran, Dutch Reformed, and Anglican (Church of England) churches joined Quaker meeting houses on the

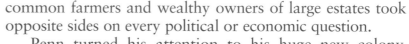

Luxurious possessions such as fine china were symbols of the good life in England and its colonies.

New Jersey attracted settlers from many nations and religions. They did not fight one another because they were too busy fighting the proprietors. Protestant churches of different denominations existed side by side. Puritans called their churches "Congregationalist" because each congregation ran its own affairs.

American Soil

When the founders of a colony encouraged new settlers to come to the colony, they wrote in glowing terms about bountiful harvests from extraordinarily fertile soil. Land was scarce in Europe and plentiful in America. The fertility of America's soil was so astonishing to people accustomed to the worn-out soil of Europe that they didn't worry about the future of the soil. But they all eventually had to face the fact that the soil's fertility was limited. Many colonists grew corn as their first and most important crop, and corn tends to deplete the soil of its nutrients quickly.

Colonial farmers planted the same crops on their land each year, until they used up the soil's natural fertility. New Jersey's soil had noticeably deteriorated by the mid-1700s. When that happened, a farmer's only choices were either to move on to new land or accept smaller crops. For example, some colonial farms could grow only 20 bushels of corn per acre. When farmers used up the fertility of their farms in the first colonies, many went west. Their new land produced 50 to 100 bushels of corn per acre, until it too was worn out. After fifty years of farming in the west, corn production declined to only 40 bushels per acre. Consider that in modern times, farmers regularly produce as many as 130 bushels per acre with the help of fertilizers.

Colonial farmers knew that soil had limits, but had little idea how to conserve it. The presence of fresh land just to the west discouraged farmers from putting great effort into conserving soil. In the 1700s, most

Settlers in America had to clear the land of trees, an almost unheard-of job in Europe. Because soil wore out, and because planting crops required a lot of labor, a farmer, even with help, could still plant only about 50 acres a season. Corn was the easiest crop to raise because it fed both people and livestock. Farmers built rail fences to keep livestock from trampling their crops.

farmers did not fertilize their fields with manure from their livestock, although there was always plenty of it available. Some believed it would make the crops taste bad. Others let their livestock into the fields after the harvest to eat the stubble: the animals cleared and fertilized the fields at the same time. A few people used lime or fish as fertilizer, a practice they learned from Native Americans. When the crops exhausted the soil, they let the field lie fallow.

With unused land so easy to find, farmers also paid no attention to the problem of soil erosion. They commonly plowed rows straight up and down hills instead of along the land's natural contours, making it easy for rain to wash the soil downhill. Rich fields of black soil gave way to rocky gullies of red clay, and clear rivers turned brown and muddy from all the soil washed into them.

streets of New Jersey towns. The proprietors publicized the advantages of their holdings with words like these: "For the Soil it is Good and capable to produce anything that England doth. ... the yearly increase is far greater. The Air Temperate and Healthy; Winter not so long as it is in England: Few Natives in the Country; but those that are, are very Peaceable, Useful, and Serviceable to the English Inhabitants."

On their farms people grew corn from a soil that yielded a harvest "considerably greater than in England." They planted orchards, raised cattle and hogs, and some grew **flax**, from which they made **linen**. Farmers and townspeople alike built brick houses as soon as they could afford them. Tradesmen readily found work in New Jersey: at sawmills, gristmills, and leather tanneries; as blacksmiths, coopers (barrel makers), carpenters, and

Above: A New Jersey mill. Grist mills used the power of flowing water to turn waterwheels, which then turned large millstones to grind grain into flour or corn into cornmeal.

Opposite, Top: Colonists who grew flax then processed fibers from the stems to make linen thread and cloth.

Opposite, Bottom: The Catholic king, James II, ruled for barely three years, from 1685 to 1688. Discontented Protestants in England wrote to James' son-in-law, William, in the Netherlands. William landed in England with an army, and James fled to France, leaving the throne to King William III and his wife, Mary II. Mary was James II's daughter and a Protestant.

bricklayers. New Jersey also had iron mines, furnaces, mills, and forges.

The death of King Charles II in 1685 gave England's throne to the Duke of York, who became King James II. As king, James II became unpopular, because he was Catholic and because he acted to increase his own authority over both England and the colonies. He tried to bypass **Parliament** in making laws. Worse, he raised **taxes** throughout the colonies and banned the colonial legislatures. He appointed Sir Edmund Andros, who had already earned the hatred of New York and New Jersey colonists, as the governor of all the New England colonies, plus New York and New Jersey.

By 1688 Andros was a virtual dictator over a mega-colony called the Dominion of New England. The proprietors of New Jersey had no choice but to submit to him. However, the Dominion of New England had a short life. King James II, after only three years in power, was

Queen Anne, the sister of the late Queen Mary II, ruled England from 1702 to 1714. She took over the government of New Jersey when it was surrendered by the proprietors.

driven from the throne and replaced by King William III and his wife, Queen Mary II. New Jersey's proprietors regained control of their holdings, but their days were numbered.

The proprietors' insistence on collecting rent from largeareas of land was their downfall. New Jersey's citizens and elected officials openly rebelled against the proprietary governments, refusing to pass or enforce laws. Mobs attacked judges and broke up court proceedings. One prominent leader of the rebellion was the wealthy, 22-year-old Lewis Morris II. He brandished a sword at the governor at a public meeting and was arrested. Morris escaped, went into hiding, and wrote letters to the town governments to stir them up against the proprietors. This young rebel was destined to be governor of New Jersey.

Groups of worried citizens wrote to London asking for a royal governor to be placed in control of the Jerseys. Desperate to restore order, 52 proprietors agreed to surrender the right of government to the Crown, provided they could keep control of land ownership. On April 15, 1702, East and West Jersey were united as a single royal colony, New Jersey. At that time, New Jersey had a total population of about 10,000, three-quarters of the people living in what had been East Jersey.

4.
TWO JERSEYS BECOME ONE

The government of New Jersey, having been surrendered by the proprietors, became part of the government of New York. New Jersey and New York were to share a royal governor, but New Jersey was to have its own appointed council and elected assembly. The assembly alternated between Burlington and Perth Amboy for its meetings. The governor chose his council from among New Jersey's many proprietors. Under the new colonial government, Christians—with the notable exception of Catholics—were granted religious liberty. One privilege retained by the proprietors was the exclusive right to buy land from the Native Americans.

THE FATE OF THE DELAWARES

The relationship between the Delawares and the Europeans had changed dramatically after the English took over the colony in 1664. From that date on, white colonists gradually crowded the Delawares out of the colony. Smallpox, malaria, and measles epidemics continued to reduce the Native American population. The surviving Delawares kept moving north and west in an effort to escape white pressure. Some moved into the northernmost corner of New Jersey and into New York. Other Delawares moved westward into Pennsylvania.

One group withdrew to the colony's south central interior, into the Pine Barrens, which the English found unappealing. The groups leader, Weequehela, was called "the King of New Jersey" by white settlers. When, in the wake of an argument, Weequehela was convicted of murder and hanged in 1727, his discouraged followers moved to the Lehigh Valley in eastern Pennsylvania.

Barely ten years later, the Delawares were driven from their refuge in Pennsylvania. A few returned to New Jersey and converted to Christianity under the influence of a Presbyterian **missionary**. In 1758 the Delawares remaining in New Jersey, now only a few hundred in number, gave up the last of their land. Some adopted European ways and lived among the colonists, and some married Native

MISSIONARY: PERSON SENT BY A CHURCH, USUALLY TO A FOREIGN LAND, TO SPREAD A RELIGION, USUALLY CHRISTIANITY

Americans from other groups and left the area. Most moved to a **reservation** on three thousand acres in the Pine Barrens. A missionary, John Brainerd, became superintendent of the reservation. Brainerd and the Christian Native Americans built a settlement on the reservation and named it Brotherton. Only sixty remained on the reservation by the time of the American Revolution. They finally moved to a reservation in New York.

Philadelphia as it appeared in 1702

Cider was made by crushing apples in a cider mill to extract their juice. Small cider mills were operated by hand, while larger ones were turned by horses.

LIFE IN THE ROYAL COLONY

The two Jerseys presented different pictures when they were united in 1702. West Jersey had been settled mostly by Quakers, whose large farms spread out along the creeks feeding into the Delaware River. Burlington had been the capital, but the great city of Philadelphia, across the river in Pennsylvania, was the center of commerce. An indentured servant in Burlington wrote, "Every house has a garden and orchard, stored with apples, peaches, and cherries. Cider is the common drink here, some houses making one hundred and fifty barrels in the year. There are two Quaker Meetings and one church … ."

East Jersey had been drawn into the orbit of New York City. Its towns developed along the seacoast and the bays and rivers, populated by colonists from a variety of nations and religions. Perth Amboy was the capital. East Jersey colonists had smaller farms than those in the west, and some pursued whaling and fishing.

The interior, with its greater distance from major

Most early houses had wood shingles, and cedar was the most water-repellent wood.

A view of New York City. New York's government argued that it had the right to tax all trading ships using New Jersey ports and tried to insist that all New Jersey–bound ships stop first in New York Harbor. This was a source of long and bitter controversy between the two colonies. The conflict ended when New Jersey became a royal colony under the control of New York's governor.

ports, and the great expanse of the Pine Barrens, did not attract settlers. However, the interior provided opportunities for income from lumber, furs, and the production of pitch, tar, and resin from pine. In addition

to lumber, New Jersey's plentiful trees provided charcoal to fire the colony's iron forges. Great cedars were dug up and pulled out of the swamps to make water-resistant shingles.

New Jersey farmers grew vegetables and fruit, wheat, corn, and other grains, as well as flax for making linen. New Jersey had enough grain, flour, and peas for export. Rice and cranberries became local specialties. Cattle, horses, and hogs all thrived on New Jersey's pastures, and many were allowed to roam in the woods. Farmers, millers, and lumber producers shipped their goods by river or sea to Philadelphia or New York. From these ports, New Jersey's surplus went to the West Indies or Europe.

New Jersey was once covered with forests, and lumber became a major product for export. Sawmills were run by the power of flowing water.

Above: New Jersey's roads connecting Philadelphia and New York were rough and often muddy. The coaches had no springs. Passengers cowered on narrow benches under the canvas top, at the mercy of the plentiful mosquitos.

Right: The College of New Jersey in Princeton, as it appeared around 1764. Its Nassau Hall temporarily housed the new United States government in 1783.

Coaches carried passengers across New Jersey on the route between New York and Philadelphia, a two-or three-day trip. The rough dirt roads of this popular route were New Jersey's first toll roads. Roadside tavern-keepers made a living by providing overnight lodging and food to the travelers.

RELIGION AND EDUCATION

By the mid-1700s, New Jersey had more than a hundred places of worship, but not all of them had ministers. Ministers were not a part of the Quaker religion. Other Christian congregations, particularly in the countryside, had to share ministers, who traveled from church to church. Dutch Reformed and Anglican ministers had to travel to Europe to become qualified, so they were in especially short supply.

As an answer to such shortages, church leaders founded two colleges as places to educate and train ministers. However, the colleges were not limited to ministerial students and also offered a more general education. New Jersey was the only colony to have two colleges within its borders. The College of New Jersey, founded in 1746 in Elizabeth, was moved to Princeton ten

years later. It eventually was renamed Princeton University. Presbyterians were active in establishing the college, although they did not control it.

A group of Dutch Reformed Church members founded Queens College in 1766, although it, too, was not church controlled. Queens College, in New Brunswick, began with a single teacher and about twenty students. It was closed while **British** troops occupied the town during the Revolutionary War, and eventually became Rutgers University long after the war.

Most towns supported a schoolhouse and a teacher to teach children to read and write. In rural areas parents sometimes pooled their resources to hire a teacher and set up a school, but country schools were few and far between. Only one town, Burlington, had a public library. New Jersey had no printing presses or newspapers.

British: NATIONALITY OF A PERSON BORN IN GREAT BRITAIN; PEOPLE BORN IN ENGLAND ARE CALLED "ENGLISH"

Students assemble inside a schoolhouse of the 1700s.

42

The People of New Jersey

When the English took over New Jersey in 1664, only a few hundred Europeans had settled on the edges of the province, which was the home of some 3,000 Native Americans. Twenty years later, the settler population had grown to about 5,000, including 300 black slaves. By 1700 this population had nearly tripled. The Native Americans population dwindled to a few hundred over the course of the next fifty years as European settlement pushed them out of New Jersey.

By the time the Revolution began, about 125,000 people lived in New Jersey. Of this number, about 44% were English, 16% Irish or Scottish, 15% Dutch, 8% German, and 8% black, most of whom were slaves. The remaining 9% were of other nationalities, such as French or Swedish. A mere sixty Native Americans lived on a New Jersey reservation.

A NEW GOVERNMENT?

New Jersey's assembly complained that the governor they shared with New York did not pay enough attention to New Jersey. The assembly members, including the famously rebellious Lewis Morris, fought each governor at every turn, and each governor dismissed the assembly and called for new elections at frequent intervals. The government accomplished very little. Finally, in 1738, after repeated appeals to London, New Jersey received its own governor, none other than Lewis Morris, now an old man of 68.

Surprisingly, Morris ruled with an iron hand and became as unpopular as his predecessors. He thought he knew how to handle uncooperative legislators, having been one himself for much of his career. The assembly voted to cut Morris's pay, and refused to pass the laws he desired. The governor and the assembly members traded insults. The colony's government ground to a halt and riots erupted over old landownership controversies. For example, when people refused to pay rent to the

Lewis Morris inherited huge estates in New Jersey and New York. He had broken with the Quakers because he found them too strict. At the time that Morris became the governor of New Jersey, the assembly tried to control governors by controlling their salaries. Wrote a member of the assembly, "Let us keep the dogs poor and we'll make them do as we please."

Philadelphia, January 6. 1734-5.

Advertisement.

THE following Tracts of Land, in the Rights of *Joseph Helby*, to be Sold by *John Sikes*, and now to be seen on the Records at *Burlington, viz.* A Tract of Land above the Branches of *Rariton*, between the River *Delaware* and the Bounds of the *Eastern* Division of *New · Jersey*, on the River *Delaware* below the Forks thereof, containing 1666 Acres. Another Tract above the Branches of *Rariton*, between the River *Delaware* and the *Eastern* Division of the said Province, on a. Branch of *Delaware* called *Paquae-fink* or the great Meadows, containing 1250 Acres. Another Tract at W*atanong* near *Whipany* in *Hunterdon* County, joining to *Joseph Kirkbride*, containing 786 Acres. Another Tract near *Cohansie* in *Salem* County in *Fenwick's* Colony, containing 170 Acres. Another Tract of Land on the W. N. W. Branch of Great *Egg-Harbour*, called *Helby's* Forest, containing 1666 Acres. Whoever inclines to purchase the whole or any Part thereof, may apply to to *Thomas Lawrence*, Esq; in *Philadelphia*, and be further informed of the Conditions of Sale, *&c.*

This advertisement offered land for sale in 1734. Much of the land in New Jersey could only be rented, and this led to rioting.

proprietors, the proprietors evicted them and jailed them for trespassing. Rioters then freed the prisoners, wrecking the jails in the process. When Morris died in 1746, the new governor, Jonathan Belcher, was no better able to control the colony, and land riots continued to occur periodically for nearly a decade.

THE FRENCH AND INDIAN WAR

England and France had a long and bitter history of rivalry and war. French colonists settled in Canada and built New

France. Its capital was Quebec. French explorers claimed all of America from the Allegheny Mountains to the Rocky Mountains and from Canada to Mexico. Few French people settled in this vast area. Instead, French traders traveled the waterways throughout this area to hunt and trap and to trade with the Native Americans. **Great Britain** and France went to war in 1755 for reasons that had nothing to do with New Jersey. The conflict came about when British settlers began pushing across the Allegheny Mountains.

The French claimed the lands where modern Pittsburgh, Pennsylvania, now stands. Virginia land speculators wanted this land. In 1753 the royal governor of Virginia sent a young **militia** officer named George Washington to tell the French to leave. The French

GREAT BRITAIN: NATION FORMED BY ENGLAND, WALES, SCOTLAND, AND NORTHERN IRELAND; "GREAT BRITAIN" CAME INTO USE WHEN ENGLAND AND SCOTLAND FORMALLY UNIFIED IN 1707.

MILITIA: A GROUP OF CITIZENS NOT NORMALLY PART OF THE ARMY WHO JOIN TOGETHER TO DEFEND THEIR LAND IN AN EMERGENCY

A colonial militia trains for combat. France and England went to war against one another four times between 1689 and 1754. During this time span, the two nations spent more than thirty years in a state of war.

ndress of Representatives 15 Jun'ry to Feb 157

To His Excellency JONATHAN BELCHER, Esq; Captain General and Governor in Chief in and over his Majesty's Province of New-Jersey, and Territories thereon depending in America, Chancellor and Vice-Admiral in the same, &c.

Au 134

The Humble ADDRESS of the Representatives of the said Province, in General Assembly met.

May it please your Excellency ;

WE, His Majesty's dutiful and loyal Subjects, the Representatives of the Colony of New-Jersey, in General Assembly conven'd, beg Leave to observe, that we have duly considered the several Letters and Petitions referred to in your Excellency's Speech.

As to the Letters from the Secretary of State, we have already anticipated the Necessity of the first of them, by granting the Supply therein mentioned, before it came to Hand ; and as to the latter of them, we acknowledge, with Gratitude, His Majesty's paternal Care, in ordering a naval Assistance for our Protection, in Case the same should be needed: And, as faithful Subjects, we have already exerted ourselves to the Utmost, for strengthening the offensive Operations against the French, even as fully as our Sovereign, by the Letter first abovementioned, has requested, without clogging the Inlistment of the Men, though their Number might have been more considerable, had not your Excellency insisted on restricting the Time for sinking the Money struck on that, and the late similar Occasions, to so short a Period, and in Case we had otherwise succeeded in our Application for a Paper Currency; being truly concerned, that our Zeal for the common Cause, should be unhappily cramped through those Obstructions; which, we promise ourselves, will be removed ; observing with Pleasure and Gratitude, His Majesty's kind Assurances, couched in His most Gracious Speech from the Throne; signifying His paternal Regard for America; His Willingness to remove any Ground of Dissatisfaction ; and recommending it to His faithful Commons, to lay the Burthens they might judge unavoidable, in such a Manner as would least distress and exhaust His People : Glorious Maxims indeed ! well worthy the Great King who has adopted them ; and highly expedient to be observed, amidst the Calamities and Confusion of War ; and we fully depend they will take Place in our Relief, as extraordinary and uncommon Events have rendered an Alleviation to our Burthen absolutely necessary.

We are of Opinion, this Colony has furnished the Carriages and Stores requisite for the King's Service, when demanded, with as great Chearfulness and Expedition as any Colony on the Continent ; and, at their own Expence, have transported the Baggage of two Regiments, receiving the Thanks of the principal Officer for the same ; and have been further honoured with his Lordship's kind Acknowledgement of their Civility and Heartiness: And it gives us great Concern, to find his Lordship should now complain of any Obstruction to the Service, which, we have Reason to suppose, must be owing to some Misrepresentations that may have been made him, as we have not heard of any real Cause of Complaint ; we hope that on Enquiry, it will appear without Foundation.

This House, truly sensible of the impending Danger brought upon his Majesty's Northern Colonies, by the ill Success of the War, have thought it their indispensable Duty to provide, by every practicable Method, for the Security of this and the neighbouring Colonies, by putting the Militia upon a good and serviceable Footing ; and we have, by a Bill now sent up to the Council, put it in the Power of

Members of the New Jersey assembly publicly aired their disagreement with the governor about collecting taxes to fund the French and Indian War.

refused, so Washington returned the next year with a small force of Virginia militia. Washington led his men in a surprise attack against the French. Washington's men killed 9 French soldiers and captured 21 more. This small victory had enormous consequences, because it started a long and deadly war between and France. The French quickly answered Washington's early victory by inflicting a series of defeats on the frontier. In Europe the war was known as the Seven Years' War. Americans called it the French and Indian War.

New Jersey was in little danger of attack during this war, but, like all the colonies, was expected to contribute money, men, and supplies to the war effort. The historically difficult assembly refused to raise taxes to support the war, but instead, after much argument, issued bonds and went into debt to provide funding. New Jersey was slow to support the war, but attacks by Native Americans along the upper Delaware River raised citizens' fears in western New Jersey. Citizens in turn convinced their elected representatives to recruit men to join the fighting. New Jersey's 1,000-man regiment, the "Jersey Blues," fought in New York, at Oswego, Lake George, and Fort Ticonderoga. Many New Jersey soldiers were captured, wounded, or killed in these battles.

5.
REVOLUTION AND STATEHOOD

The British defeated the French at Quebec in 1759 and later took control of Canada. In 1763 France and Great Britain signed a peace treaty giving the British control of much of North America east of the Mississippi River. Also in 1763 a 33-year-old lawyer, William Franklin, was named royal governor of New Jersey. The son of the prominent Pennsylvanian, Benjamin Franklin, William had fought with the Pennsylvania militia, traveled to England with his distinguished father, and had inherited his father's gift for getting along with people. A wise and cautious man, Franklin was able to work with the competing factions and keep the government functioning.

The costly war with France had convinced the British government that the colonies should help pay the costs of sending soldiers to America to defend colonists against Native Americans. Parliament imposed taxes on the colonists, and this enraged them. People throughout the colonies believed that a distant Parliament had no right to tax them and was violating their right to self-government.

The first major new tax law was the Sugar Act of 1764. The act called for import and export duties, or taxes, to be paid on many trade goods, such as sugar, coffee, indigo, and animal hides. The British sent royal navy ships to patrol the American coast and enforce the law. They also assigned customs officials to collect the taxes and had merchants arrested who were thought to be evading the taxes. Most of New Jersey's trade passed through New York or Philadelphia, but the more aggressive enforcement of tax collection led to a reduction in trade in these ports and a shortage of money in New Jersey.

Next, in 1765 Parliament passed the Stamp Act. Under the Stamp Act, colonists had to pay to have most documents stamped, or risk arrest. Even newspapers had to have stamps. The Stamp Act affected colonists of all social classes. Resistance grew, and groups calling themselves the Sons of Liberty were organized throughout the colonies to organize protests and sabotage any efforts to enforce the Stamp Act. The Sons of Liberty had several

Revolutionary Benjamin Franklin was hurt by his son's decision to remain loyal to Great Britain. He wrote to William, "You ... see everything with government eyes." Father and son eventually reconciled after the Revolution, but some ill feeling remained.

ACT: LAW, SO CALLED BECAUSE IT IS MADE BY AN ACT OF GOVERNMENT

thousand members in New Jersey. They threatened attacks on the offices and homes of anyone who tried to use the stamps. The New Jersey stamp tax collector quickly resigned, fearing violence. New Jersey lawyers met and decided to refuse to use the stamps. The assembly met informally at a tavern and appointed several men to attend the Stamp Act Congress, a protest meeting held in New York. Although Governor Franklin wanted to enforce Parliament's laws, he decided not to interfere and risk making enemies among the protesters.

So unpopular was the Stamp Act that Parliament repealed it in March 1766. Still, the king insisted that Great Britain's Parliament had the right to make laws for the colonies and collect taxes. Parliament passed a new set of laws taxing even more products, and angering more colonists. Tensions continued to grow between colonists and British soldiers and officials.

Since the colonies were forbidden to produce their own money, they had to rely on foreign coins, such as these silver coins from Spain. Such coins were in especially short supply in New Jersey, where more goods were imported than exported.

Colonial men gathered in coffeehouses and taverns to exchange ideas about politics and rebellion.

PATRIOTS: AMERICANS WHO WANTED THE COLONIES TO BE INDEPENDENT FROM GREAT BRITAIN

BOYCOTT: AN AGREEMENT TO REFUSE TO BUY FROM OR SELL TO CERTAIN BUSINESSES OR PEOPLE

At the suggestion of Virginia **patriots**, the leaders of opposition to British laws formed Committees of Correspondence throughout the colonies. By writing letters, the Committees would keep one another informed and make plans for the colonies to cooperate. They also planned to spread news that would influence public opinion in favor of rebellion. The Committees got all the colonies except New Hampshire to **boycott** British merchandise. The boycott convinced the British to repeal most taxes, except for the tax on tea, by 1770.

FROM BOYCOTT TO BATTLEFIELD

Relieved of tax burdens for a while, the colonies prospered, and colonial life remained calm until 1773. Few colonists really wanted independence from Great Britain, as long as they could make their own laws and set

their own taxes. Then Parliament passed a law that gave one British tea seller, the struggling East India Company, special treatment. The East India Company was given a monopoly in the colonies, so that it could sell its tea more cheaply than any other dealer. Once again, the Committees of Correspondence went to work, spreading word of the new law and the coming East India Company tea shipments. The Sons of Liberty organized actions against the shipments.

As rebellion grew ever more likely, patriots gathered in public to support their cause. The United States Constitution protects the right of citizens to assemble in public.

The first such action, the famous Boston Tea Party, occurred in December 1773 with the dumping of a large tea shipment into Boston Harbor. Actions in other port cities followed, including one in Greenwich, New Jersey, where protesters dressed as Native Americans burned a shipload of tea. Soon after, the New Jersey assembly and several counties voted to create Committees of Correspondence. When Britain responded to the Boston Tea Party by closing the port of Boston and placing Massachusetts under military rule, many in the colonies began to argue that they would have to fight for independence from Great Britain. Governor Franklin, staunchly loyal to Great Britain, refused to call the assembly into session, so the assembly met informally and voted to send delegates to a meeting of the colonies in Philadelphia. This September 1774 meeting became known as the First Continental Congress.

The congress drew up a set of resolutions stating the rights of the colonies to self-government and formed a Continental Association to boycott British trade goods and organize local governments. Finally, the delegates agreed to meet again in May 1775. The New Jersey assembly voted unanimously to send delegates to the second congress. Before the second congress met, the first battle of the American Revolution had been fought in Lexington and Concord, Massachusetts, on April 19, 1775. The Second Continental Congress voted to raise a Continental Army, with George Washington as its commander-in-chief.

At the same time, local committees of patriots in New Jersey set up a separate elected government called the Provincial Congress. This Congress met in Trenton and voted for a tax to create and arm a patriot militia. Meanwhile, in November 1775, Governor Franklin called the old assembly into session and urged it to vote against independence from Great Britain. The assembly complied, but that meeting proved to be its last. The Provincial Congress took over the government of New Jersey. One of its acts was to remove the property ownership requirement for voting. New Jersey became one of a handful of states that allowed all tax paying adult white men to vote regardless of whether they owned land.

Although the Provincial Congress supported the war for independence, New Jersey's citizens were deeply divided into two camps, patriot and **loyalist**. The Provincial Congress decided to arrest the loyalist governor, and Franklin was sent to Connecticut as a prisoner of war. The Provincial Congress also chose a new set of delegates to the Continental Congress. The five delegates all signed the Declaration of Independence on July 4, 1776. Two days earlier, on July 2, New Jersey's Provincial Congress approved a state constitution.

New Jersey was both barracks and battleground for the duration of the Revolutionary War. George Washington

Governor William Franklin grew bitter over his arrest and imprisonment. Released in 1778, he became a loyalist leader in British-occupied New York City. At the end of the war, he sailed for England, where he lived for the rest of his life.

Opposite Top: Francis Hopkinson (left) and John Witherspoon (right), two of the five New Jersey men who signed the Declaration of Independence. Hopkinson, a former colonial councilman, composed religious music in his spare time. Witherspoon was a minister who came from Scotland to serve as president of Princeton in 1768. The other three signers (not pictured) were the lawyer and councilman Richard Stockton, the farmer John Hart, and Abraham Clark, a farmer, surveyor, and sheriff.

Left: William Livingston served as the first governor of the state of New Jersey, from 1776 until he died in 1790. Unlike many of his predecessors, he was so well respected that he won re-election to the office every year.

and the Continental Army retreated straight across New Jersey in the dark days after the British captured New York. Washington boldly launched a surprise Christmas Eve attack and defeated the British at Trenton, and soon after at Princeton. The Continental army went into winter quarters at Morristown, the first of three winters spent in New Jersey, while the British army was forced into a small area on the coast.

The Revolutionary War brought tremendous property damage and disruption of lives in New Jersey. Soldiers from both armies raided New Jersey farms for food. While under British occupation, thousands of New Jersey citizens had declared themselves to be loyalists. Loyalists raised a volunteer militia, and skirmishes erupted between gangs of patriots and loyalists, as neighbor turned against neighbor. Hundreds of New Jersey loyalists had their property confiscated and moved to Canada, especially Nova Scotia, after the war. Some moved to England.

Opposite: George Washington and his army made the dangerous crossing of the icy Delaware River on Christmas night 1776 so that they could surprise the enemy while they were distracted by holiday celebrations. The plan was an outstanding success.

Above: The legend of Molly Pitcher arose from the battle of Monmouth, New Jersey. It was probably based on one of the women who brought pitchers of water to the thirsty Continental soldiers. The woman known to history as Molly Pitcher is said to have taken her husband's place at his cannon when he fell wounded.

Right: The Battle of Trenton, early morning December 26, 1776, arguably the turning point of the Revolution.

EPILOGUE

After the Revolution Princeton served as the nation's capital for a few months in 1783. The Continental Congress met at the college, and George Washington attended to supervise the disbanding of his army. The following year, the congress met at Trenton, and chose Trenton to be the future national capital, but in the end the national government went to New York City, and then to Washington, D.C. New Jersey became the third state to adopt the U.S. Constitution on December 18, 1787. Trenton became the capital of New Jersey.

New Jersey has more than 8 million people, of whom about 13 percent are black. The state population also includes Asian Americans, about 6 percent of the total, and Hispanic Americans, about 13percent of the total. New Jersey is a densely populated state, with about 1,000

The New Jersey state constitution of 1776 uniquely granted the right to vote to "all inhabitants." As a result, New Jersey's women were the only women in the United States permitted to vote during the nation's early years.

people per square mile of land area. Three out of four people live in cities such as Camden, Elizabeth, Jersey City, Newark, Paterson, and Trenton. Many leave the state each day when they commute to work in New York City or Philadelphia. Only 1 percent of New Jersey's workers are involved in farming. Twenty percent work in manufacturing, many producing chemicals, medicines, and electronic goods, or processing foods. New Jersey has a notable transportation network, including toll roads, railroads, bridges, and tunnels into New York City, seaports, and airports.

Beyond the metropolitan areas, about 40 percent of the state's land area is covered with hardwood forests. Such animals as deer, foxes, skunks, possum, raccoons, and minks still live in New Jersey. Waterfowl and shellfish abound on the coast. The unique Pine Barrens are protected by the million-acre Pinelands National Reserve, established in 1978. The pinelands are the home to rare species of plants

Right: New Jersey's Great Swamp provides a perfect habitat for waterfowl. Over 675,000 acres of this densely forested marshland have been preserved as a national wildlife refuge.

Main picture: The beaches of New Jersey attract migrating birds and human visitors.

and animals, including rare orchids, insect-eating plants, and a unique species of tree frog. Towns and farms within the reserve hold more than half a million people, but the reserve protects the area from further development. Blueberries and cranberries are harvested from the pinelands.

The ocean beaches of New Jersey's coast attract numerous visitors. Atlantic City, with its boardwalk and casinos, is nationally famous. New Jersey shares with Pennsylvania the beautiful Delaware Water Gap National Recreation Area, which spans the upper reaches of the Delaware River. The Statue of Liberty, known to countless visitors to New York City, is located on a small island very close to New Jersey. Visitors can get to the island from either Jersey City or Manhattan.

Waterloo Village, near Stanhope, offers reconstructed colonial and Delaware Native American villages. Monmouth Battlefield State Park and Morristown National Historical Park preserve important Revolutionary War sites.

Below: Hunterdon County's Clinton Mill in northwestern New Jersey now houses the Clinton Historical Museum.

DATELINE

1524: Giovanni da Verrazano explores the coast of what will become New Jersey.

1609: Henry Hudson explores the modern-day Hudson River and visits the coast of New Jersey.

1660: Dutch settlers establish the town of Bergen, the first permanent European settlement in New Jersey.

1664: England conquers New Netherland, and the king gives the land to his brother, the Duke of York. The Duke of York transfers ownership of New Jersey to Sir George Carteret and Lord Berkeley.

1665: Philip Carteret arrives in New Jersey to serve as governor.

1665–1667: English settlers found six new towns in New Jersey, including Newark and Elizabethtown.

1674: Lord Berkeley sells his half share of New Jersey to Quakers. This leads to the division of the province into East Jersey and West Jersey.

1681: After the death of George Carteret, East Jersey becomes the property of 24 owners.

1688–1692: New Jersey becomes part of the Dominion of New England.

1702: East and West Jersey's many proprietors surrender control of the colony to England, and the two halves are reunited as New Jersey.

1738: Lewis Morris becomes royal governor of New Jersey, the first royal governorship that is not shared with New York.

1746: The College of New Jersey, later to become Princeton University, is established.

1758: The last Delaware Native Americans in New Jersey move to a reservation in the Pine Barrens.

1776: New Jersey's revolutionary government arrests loyalist Governor William Franklin. New Jersey approves a state constitution. William Livingston becomes the first governor of the state of New Jersey. George Washington and the Continental army win an inspiring victory at the Battle of Trenton.

DECEMBER 18, 1787: New Jersey becomes the third state to ratify the United States Constitution.

Glossary

ACT: law, so called because it is made by an act of government

AMERICA: land that contains the continents of North America and South America

ANGLICAN: belonging to the Church of England, a Protestant church and the state church of England

ASSEMBLY: lower house of a legislature, with delegates elected by the voters

BARRENS: tract of land on which little of commercial value can be grown

BOYCOTT: agreement to refuse to buy from or sell to certain businesses or people

BRITISH: nationality of a person born in Great Britain; people born in England are called "English"

CATHOLIC: Roman Catholic; the oldest Christian church organization, governed by authorities based in Rome

CHARTER: document containing the rules for running an organization

COLONY: land owned and controlled by a distant nation; a colonist is a permanent settler of a colony

DUTCH: nationality of people born in the Netherlands

EPIDEMIC: widespread outbreak of contagious disease

FLAX: plant grown for its seeds, from which linseed oil is made, and its stem, which provides fibers for making linen

GREAT BRITAIN: nation formed by England, Wales, Scotland, and Northern Ireland; "Great Britain" came into use when England and Scotland formally unified in 1707.

INDENTURED SERVANT: person who has agreed to work as a servant for a certain number of years in exchange for food, clothing, a place to sleep, and payment of one's passage across the Atlantic to the colonies

INDIANS: name given to Native Americans at the time Europeans first came to America, because it was believed that America was actually a close neighbor of India

LINEN: thread or cloth made from the fibers of flax stems

LOYALIST: colonist who wanted America to remain a colony of Great Britain

MILITIA: group of citizens not normally part of the army who join together to defend their land in an emergency

MISSIONARY: person sent by a church, usually to a foreign land, to spread a religion, usually Christianity

NATIVE AMERICANS: people who had been living in America for thousands of years at the time that the first Europeans arrived

NETHERLANDS: European nation formed by the union of several provinces, including Holland. Amsterdam is the capital city.

PARLIAMENT: legislature of Great Britain

PATRIOTS: Americans who wanted the colonies to be independent from Great Britain

PERSECUTION: punishing people because of their beliefs, religion, or race

PROPRIETOR: private owner

PROTESTANT: member of any Christian church that has broken away from the Roman Catholic or Eastern Orthodox Churches

PURITANS: Protestants who wanted the Church of England to practice a more "pure" form of Christianity, and established a colony in New England

QUAKER: originally a term of mockery given to members of the Society of Friends, a Christian group founded in England around 1650

RESERVATION: tract of land reserved by the government as a dwelling place for Native Americans

TAX: payment required by the government

TOWN MEETING: basis of local government in New England, in which voting citizens met and conducted town business as a group

WEST INDIES: islands of the Caribbean Sea, so called because the first European visitors thought they were near India

FURTHER READING

Doherty, Kieran. *William Penn, Quaker Colonist*. Brookfield, Conn.: Millbrook Press, 1998.

Quiri, Patricia R. *The Algonquians*. Danbury, Conn.: Franklin Watts, 1992.

Smith, Carter, ed. *Daily Life: A Source Book on Colonial America*. Brookfield, Conn.: Millbrook Press, 1991.

Smith, Carter, ed. *The Revolutionary War: A Source Book on Colonial America*. Brookfield, Conn.: Millbrook Press, 1991.

WEBSITES

www.americaslibrary.gov
Select "Jump back in time" for links to history activities.

http://www.thinkquest.org/library
Explore links to numerous student-designed sites about American colonial history.

http://www.state.nj.us/pinelands/
The official site of the New Jersey Pinelands Commission; it includes historical information and games.

http://www.state.nj.us/hangout_nj/
The official New Jersey site for kids has cartoon histories and games.

http://www.delawaretribeofindians.nsn.us/
This site run by the Delaware Native Americans, contains information about the tribe for Native Americans and others.

Disclaimer
All Internet addresses (URLs) given in this book were valid at the time it went to press. However, due to the dynamic nature of the Internet, some addresses may have changed, or sites may have ceased to exist since publication. While the author and publisher regret any inconvenience this may cause readers, no responsibility for any such changes can be accepted by either the author or the publisher.

BIBLIOGRAPHY

The American Heritage History of the Thirteen Colonies. New York: American Heritage, 1967.

Hawke, David Freeman. *Everyday Life in Early America.* New York: Harper & Row, 1988.

McCormick, Richard P. *New Jersey: From Colony to State, 1609–1789.* Newark: New Jersey Historical Society, 1981.

Middleton, Richard. *Colonial America: A History, 1607–1760.* Cambridge, Mass.: Blackwell, 1992.

Myers, Albert Cook. *Narratives of Early Pennsylvania, West New Jersey, and Delaware: 1630–1707.* New York: Charles Scribner's Sons, 1912.

Pomfret, John E. *Colonial New Jersey: A History.* New York: Charles Scribner's Sons, 1973.

Taylor, Alan. *American Colonies.* New York: Viking, 2001.

INDEX